My Book About

Tiger
Woods

Concept: Jacquelyn Lynn
Cover design: Jerry D. Clement
Cover photo: Sports Images | Dreamstime.com
Interior design & production: Tuscawilla Creative Services, LLC

Tuscawilla Creative Services
CreateTeachInspire.com

For a complete list of My Book About titles, visit WriteMyBookAbout.com

For bulk orders, contact info@contacttcs.com.

Photographs licensed through Dreamstime.com

This publication is intended for entertainment purposes only.

ISBN: 978-1-941826-39-3

How to Use this Book

Do you have something to say about Tiger Woods?

Here's an opportunity to write your book about one of the greatest golfers of all time.

This book includes a mix of lined and blank pages so you can write or draw. It's also illustrated with photos you can write captions for or just use for inspiration.

Not sure what to write? Check the next page for a list of ideas.

Fill in your name on the title page, add a dedication, then turn to page 13 and begin writing.

You can fill in the table of contents as you go or when you've finished.

Finally, if you would prefer that no one else sees these instructions, carefully remove this page from the book. We recommend using an exacto knife.

Now you're ready to proudly display *My Book About Tiger Woods*.

Need some ideas to help you get started?
Write your thoughts on:

- Tiger's childhood growing up as a golf prodigy.

- Tiger as a husband, father, friend.

- The influence of his parents in his life as a youngster and an adult.

- Tiger's health challenges.

- His relationship with his fans.

- His relationship with his caddies.

- The charity work that Tiger does as an individual and through his foundation.

- How he has dealt with having his personal life made public.

- The contributions Tiger has made to the sport of golf.

- His record in major tournaments.

- His performance in the Ryder Cup and the President's Cup.

- The impact of Tiger's sponsorship deals on the success of the companies he represents.

- Your thoughts on Tiger's future.

My Book About

Tiger Woods

By

_____

Dedication

_____

_____

_____

_____

_____

_____

_____

_____

_____

_____

Contents

Photo: © Michael Bush | Dreamstime.com

Photo: © James Phelps | Dreamstime.com

_____

_____

_____

_____

_____

_____

_____

_____

_____

_____

_____

_____

_____

_____

_____

Photo: © Wirestock | Dreamstime.com

Photo: © Ali87cat | Dreamstime.com

_____

_____

_____

_____

_____

_____

_____

_____

_____

_____

_____

_____

_____

_____

_____

_____

_____

Photo: © Michael Bush | Dreamstime.com

_____

_____

_____

_____

_____

_____

_____

_____

_____

_____

_____

_____

_____

_____

_____

_____

_____

Photo: © Droopydogajna | Dreamstime.com

Photo: © Karen Foley | Dreamstime.com

_____

_____

_____

_____

_____

_____

_____

_____

_____

_____

_____

_____

_____

_____

_____

_____

Photo: © Michael Bush | Dreamstime.com

_____

_____

_____

_____

_____

_____

_____

_____

_____

_____

_____

_____

_____

_____

_____

_____

_____

_____

_____

_____

_____

_____

_____

_____

_____

_____

_____

_____

_____

_____

_____

_____

_____

_____

_____

_____

Photo: © Droopydogajna | Dreamstime.com

110 | *My Book About*

Photo: © Sports Images | Dreamstime.com

_____

_____

_____

_____

_____

_____

_____

_____

_____

_____

_____

_____

_____

_____

Photo: © Jerry Coli | Dreamstime.com

Photo: © Michael Bush | Dreamstime.com

Photo: © Ali87cat | Dreamstime.com

Photo: © Photogolpher | Dreamstime.com

_____
_____
_____
_____
_____
_____
_____
_____
_____
_____
_____
_____
_____
_____
_____
_____

Photo: © Jerry Coli | Dreamstime.com

Other Titles in the *My Book About* Series

Get a complete list of available titles:

WriteMyBookAbout.com

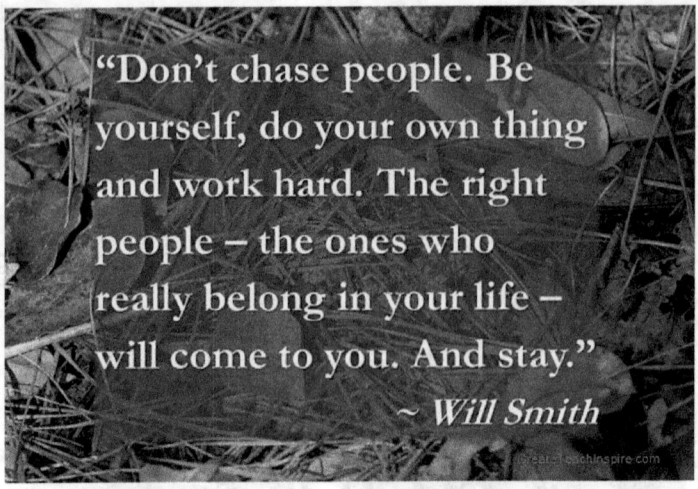

"Don't chase people. Be yourself, do your own thing and work hard. The right people – the ones who really belong in your life – will come to you. And stay."
~ *Will Smith*

"I often warn people: Somewhere along the way, someone is going to tell you, 'There is no "I" in team.' What you should tell them is, 'Maybe not. But there is an "I" in independence, individuality and integrity."

- *George Carlin*

"In a survey of 90-year-olds, when asked what they would have done differently, they responded, 'Risk more, reflect more and leave a legacy that matters.'"

- *Dr. Linda Livingstone*
Dean of Pepperdine University Business School

10 Seconds of Inspiration

Get images like these delivered to your inbox every Saturday morning. Enjoy and share!

Visit

CreateTeachInspire.com/ss

to join Shareable Saturday

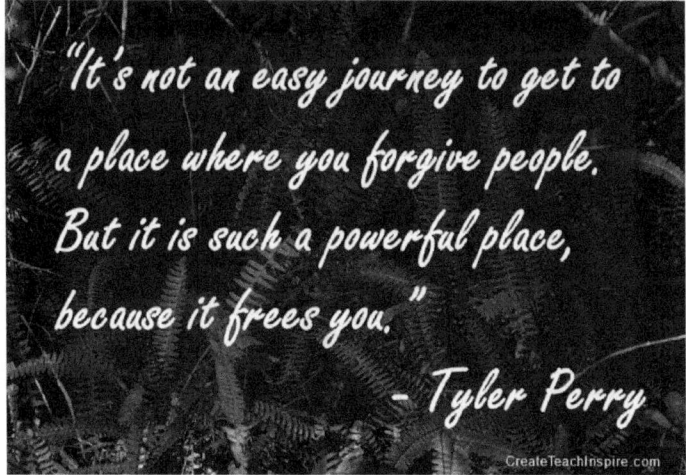

"You cannot get through a single day without having an impact on the world around you. What you do makes a difference, and you have to decide what kind of difference you want to make."

– Jane Goodall

CreateTeachInspire.com

"It's not an easy journey to get to a place where you forgive people. But it is such a powerful place, because it frees you."

– Tyler Perry

CreateTeachInspire.com

A great way to wrap up your week!

Visit **CreateTeachInspire.com/ss** to join Shareable Saturday